PRIME MOVER

P·R·I·M·E M·O·V·E·R
POEMS 1981–1985

Paul Mariani

THE GROVE PRESS POETRY SERIES
EDITED BY ROBERT PACK

GROVE PRESS, INC./NEW YORK

Some of these poems have previously appeared in the following
periodicals to whose editors grateful acknowledgment is made: *The
Agni Review, il Cobald, Hubbub, The Hudson Review, The New
England Review/Bread Loaf Quarterly, The Massachusetts Review,
The New Criterion, New Letters, Sun Dog, The Swallow's Tail,
Tendril, TriQuarterly Review, Verse.*

First Grove Press Edition 1985
First Printing 1985
ISBN: 0-394-55015-3
Library of Congress Catalog Card Number: 85-14838

First Evergreen Edition 1985
First Printing 1985
ISBN: 0-394-62083-6
Library of Congress Catalog Card Number: 85-14838

Book design by Frederica Templeton

Printed in the United States of America

GROVE PRESS, INC., 196 West Houston Street, New York, N.Y. 10014

1 3 5 4 2

FOR EILEEN

in the steady, fierce alembic,
in the wombshaped retort,
etched against the insistent dark,
something redolent of autumn gold
was surely gathering

The First Moevere of the cause above,
Whan he first made the faire cheyne of love,
Greet was th'effect, and heigh was his entente.
Wel wiste he why, and what thereof he mente;
For with that faire cheyne of love he bond
The fyr, the eyr, the water, and the lond
In certeyn boundes, that they may nat flee.

Chaucer's reading of Boethius's
On the Consolation of Philosophy

Why, tears! is it? tears; such a melting, a madrigal start!
　　Never-eldering revel and river of youth,
What can it be, this glee? the good you have there of your own?

Hopkins, *The Wreck of the Deutschland*

The empyrean, which is not spatial at all,
does not move and has no poles. It girds,
with light and love, the primum mobile,
the utmost and swiftest of the material heavens.
Angels are manifested in the primum mobile.

William Kennedy, *Ironweed*

CONTENTS

Right and Left   ix

I

New York: Sunday Morning, March 1944   3
The Box   5
Matadero, Riley & Company   8
Promises   12
A Bad Joke   14
On the Edge of the Atlantic   16
Sarcophagus   18
Light Streaming Into the Head   21

II

News That Stays News   27
The Assassins   29
Pentecost Sunday: Howard Beach   30
Loss of Life   32
Winter Meditation   34
On the Sublime   36
Ulysses Weeps   38
A Break in the Weather   40
Lines I Told Myself I Wouldn't Write   42

III

Q/A   49
Palimpsest   51
Some Sort of Answer   53
The Ghost   56
North/South   58
Minneapolis: At the Summer Solstice   60
The Sign   62
Cleaning Out the Cellar   64

IV

Goodnight Irene 69
The Ring 72
The Tern's Eye 74
The Lure 77
Prime Mover 78

V

The Eastern Point Meditations 83

Then Sings My Soul 97

RIGHT AND LEFT

In Winslow Homer's final masterpiece
it is the duck's gold eye alone
flares out against the cold Atlantic's
nauseous overwhelming greens.
Alive, the eye stares out at us in terror
as soon it will simply stare.

As you stare back into the picture
you come to almost cross
some final threshold: two ducks, right, left,
one already hit and falling
headlong to the water, its gold eye
glazed and leaded over black.

Still, the other struggles to escape,
perhaps already hit,
perhaps already dead. It hangs suspended
from the picture, as in
a still-life Audubon, the bead already drawn
for the artist's execution.

A greybrown shadow rises from the water.
We read the flash of red
as the shadow of a hunter and at last as Death
the hunter, the berry drop
the second blast of the double-barreled
shotgun. The greygreen waters

rise halfway to meet the greygreen sky
and yawn until at last
the icy whitecaps come to look
like jaggèd teeth.
And then at once it dawns: the gun
is aimed at us

as Homer meant it should. The shot,
which no one sees, has struck
the one and is about to strike the other,
and then, a bare year later,
the now-dead Homer, and now the one
who reads aright the picture.

·**I**·

NEW YORK: SUNDAY MORNING, MARCH 1944

I would walk after him into the deckle-
edged shadows rushing brightly
over Second Avenue, the iron gates
stretched taut against the sullen
storefront windows aglare in the long
dead silence of a Sunday morning
back those forty years ago.

In my smallpeaked camelcolored cap
and sailorboy blue coat I would wade
pigeontoed into the shallows of the morning's
shadow-brilliant light. I held tight
my papa's hand, my giant papa, who was
so tall and strong, as he strode against
the frowning laughter of our morning.

Gargoyles atop the tall cathedral plashed
and chattered while I kept watch
for what I knew was out there in the darkness
of the Fifty-ninth Street underpass waiting
for a knock-kneed kid to scramble by alone.
At last we saw the spangled sun lift high
above the backbent scudding clouds

like a priest king slowly rising toward
his altar. Old men dressed in vests
and jackets sat on straightbacked
broken chairs, mouthing words
I could not understand. I crept closer
to my papa then for comfort until
I heard the same sounds spilling

3

from the place I knew his mouth had been.
It was a goatfoot dance they did together,
the old men and my papa, as they clattered
on the broken Sunday pavement, growing bronzen
in a sun become the color of polenta.
My papa, who would soon be off to war,
had brought along his blond-haired, first-born,

half-Italian son to pay respects
before he had to leave the moly-scented world
of his fathers. The men were peering at the son
and laughing now, but all the boy could do
was cringe against his father's feathered,
scaly knees. And now he saw the blanched
and stricken sun begin to fall before the massed,

the scumbled clouds which the tenements had hidden
up till then. The men had dimmed to shadows
roosting in the mottled sycamores. The boy
could hear the rustling of their feathers
and the strop of talons on the trembling branches
as they turned to fix their lidless stares
upon the one the dark had summoned.

THE BOX

I sift through the battered shoebox:
thirty years of family snapshots
ripped from the five black scrapbooks
and tossed —some here, some in the garbage—
when my parents ended it at last.

A face, then half a face, flickers
from the bottom of the box: patches
of pooled light housed in the tabernacle
of the once familiar household gods, that box
broken now, the faces half-erased by rain.

A formal photo of a boy in tie and knickers,
the jacket borrowed from a neighbor:
black and black and black. The white glare
of the artist's indoor lamp rises off
the garden backdrop to form a kind of halo.

The buck-toothed smile is radiant, the hair
is tamed by vaseline and brush. About
his fingers the photographer has twined
a rosary, connoting piety. Surely
he has pleased his parents as he steps across

the threshold into this special hostwhite day.
May or early June of '47, the gothic pile
shouldering the brownstones and the shrouded
outline of the Fifty-ninth Street Bridge.
I try to warm the picture into life.

A sea of dark pews, the giant colddark pillars,
the aisle leading to the ivory marble altar,
and then the sounds of children sniffling
amidst the magisterial silence of the white-
and-black-robed sisters, the clacking black beads

looped around their waists. A tall nun
in steel-rimmed glasses sounds her clicker
and the children rise together from their kneelers.
Another click and now the voices throng about me.
And though I have been forbidden to join

my voice to the Della Robbia choir
of bellcheeked angels, I may move my lips
in union with the others. By twos —a boy,
a girl— we move as we have been taught
for months to move: small steps, *lente, lente,*

hands together, looking neither left
nor right. And now our children's army
parts the waves of half-familiar faces
either side of us as we work our way
by moonsteps to the altar . . . .

Oh to lock a moment on this momentary
clearing, before the waves crash swirling back
and in to drown the drifting mind. Step
by fumbling step we keep moving down
the aisle. A tall man winks. A lady

in a bright coat beams. I try to seem
transfixed and fix my white attention
on the young priest or the old.
In the thirty-five years since I first began
processing down the aisle God has not aged

a minute. The altar rail draws nearer.
Ten years past the midpoint of our threescore
years and ten, so that now I can see at last
the casket hunkered there before the altar.
It is polished black and has brass handles

and has a name in brass. The time will come
when I will touch its cold black edge
and then stare down into the half-familiar
face lying in the box, a formal portrait
from which all the names have been erased.

MATADERO, RILEY & COMPANY

A perfectly useless concentration:
the way one poet put it, describing
the state of the art. And what good,
this Good Friday, to stir up cold ash
to find this single image glowing:
the one circling the other like a jackal,
hackles bristling, his left fist feinting
first then slamming to his heart's content.

For the past two days troubled by Riley's
shifting image, faster than the bull-
necked Matadero, jabbing again and yet
again at the bloody head, playing it
like a cat clawing at a shredded ball.
I still see myself watching
from the safety of my front lawn, eyes fixed
across the street, my left hand gripping

the cold handlebars of my battered
Schwinn, the wobbly kickstand trying
to support it, my right arm cradling
the bag of groceries for my mother.
I stare at the solid ring of boys
watching Riley and Matadero,
expanding and contracting
like a pumping heart to let Matadero

stumble as he needs. Only
the crack of Riley's fists against
the other's face breaks the silence.
I would make more sense of all
of this, but the names are gone,
even from the small black-and-white
Kodak shots I have of them,
though one (which face I cannot now

remember) is a cop out on the Island
and another sells sneakers down
in Tampa, and one's a coach and one
did time my brother tells me for breaking
someone's neck in a barroom down in Merrick,
and two at least are dead. Most
of them are married now (and some of them
divorced) with teenage children of

their own: working class stiffs
who bought the dream without the substance—
myself among them if they would count
me in—the wops, the poles, the micks
giving way with time up and down
the sycamore and maple-tented streets
to even newer families with names
like Rodriguez, Alicea, and Rivera.

A shadow world only, and yet
the scars still itch. The eyes close
again in tired meditation and again

they flinch before that grin of Matadero's,
who waited for me as I clambered up
the far steps of the piss-soaked
tunnel running under the Long
Island railroad tracks, that graffiti-

riddled rite of adolescent passage.
How often I used to pray for him
to die. At least to be delivered
from his grip. And then, with the clear-
eyed logic of some Jacobean tragedy,
here was Riley catching up at last
with Matadero and jabbing at
his face, again, again. And this

was no clean, first-strike John
Wayne kill, the kind I once saw
a cheetah make in *Life*, when his teeth
and jaws crunched the cornered baboon's
skull. No, this was cat-and-mouse,
a jab, a jab and then another,
while the arms of Matadero hung,
too bone-weary useless to keep even

the blows from landing on his bleeding
eyes, his broken nose, disfigured
lips. On that cold March morning
back there thirty years ago,
while the random clouds drifted
piecemeal overhead, the age of Riley
replaced the short-lived age of Matadero.
And yet, what pleasure in revenge?

For months after Riley and company
pursued the beaten loser, left now
without a friend. Even I walked about
in Riley's shadow with impunity.
But in the white waste of time it all
sinks down again to *ecce homo*,
behold one more human being beaten,
this one on the playing fields of Mineola.

PROMISES

To keep from killing him, my friend had said,
I had to take apart the old horse pistol
Pappy'd given me, lock, stock and barrel, and hide
the gleaming pieces like so many Easter eggs

each which way about the house. The murderous
soft drawl of this Missouri man, who loves his words,
his wife, his two sweet sons, *and* his bourbon.
In Arkansas, the kid from Fort Worth told me,

you can still get plenty of those clean,
unadulterated killings. Take the cute little
co-ed blew half her boyfriend's face away
over some quip he'd made about the father

of her unborn babe. The kid kept five bullets
in the chambers, leaving one behind the pin
a blank, in case the car went dead down
on the Pig Trail on his way to Little Rock.

For a halfbaked Yankee who knows a little Faulkner,
Smith and Dickey, I think I got the message straight
the first time through this state. You know
how deep it goes in all of us, though it gets hidden

less down here, the dark substrata of the collective
self the more exposed, as Merton came to see
from his Cistercian cell there in Kentucky.
He also knew the North was even sicker. Remember

the Puerto Rican street gang leader, red bandana
tied about his pony hair Apache style, dawdling
that awesome Magnum for the cameras, before he fired
into those South Bronx buildings across the roof?

The kids up the road from here in rural western Mass,
shotguns straddled across their arms, stalking game
through the smoky autumn grasses, my neighbor's dog
discovered disentrailed along the gravel ditch?

Remember stumbling up the walkway past the bleeding
lenten purple iris clumps, feeling way down, low,
relieved in only this: that I couldn't tear upstairs
into the attic, clawing down under the loose boards

for my instant answer, some silverplated promise
of a jackpot zero armageddon, the scattered limbs
of the thunder-making goddess reassembled quick:
a stroke, a fingering and then the coming blast.

A BAD JOKE

Because they had to cut deep
to get the cancer in his throat,
my father-in-law was wheezing out

this joke in his old stage manner,
the one about the woman who tells
the butcher to keep on slicing

till he's halfway through
the roast beef before she tells him
dat's good dankyou now she'll take

the next two pieces. I took him
by the arm as we crossed the street,
one eye on the lookout for idiots

peeling up the avenue, the other
on those hip-cracking ice slicks
(the Christmas sun up over

the new high-risers useless
to stop the stupid wind from moaning
off the ocean) and thinking

all the while of my fifteen-year-old
son, whose voice is boom-bellowing
into manhood now and who just last week

was joking at the kitchen table
when all at once I could see
his lanky frame start shaking

as the thing crawled crab-like
over him again: his fear of turning
into elements the way the brilliant

lemur-snouted kid in Chem class
told him happens when you die,
so that I had to grab him

by the elbow as he pushed past
my chair to hold him, his rib-cage
heaving as I told him not to worry

while he had his old man there
to help him, for which white lie,
or worse, bad joke, I beg him

some day to forgive me.

ON THE EDGE OF THE ATLANTIC

An old man walking on the beach alone.
And again the high waves surged and smashed
themselves against the winter beach and rose
and hurled their weight fullforce against
the dock and seawall and rose and fell again.

He kept watch for the angry gulls who wheeled
and cried and dipped, one wing cutting
at the moiling flood for food. Early Sunday
morning and the stranding beach and him, grey air
becoming one by now with the crushed grey

saltstinging water. After so long to rest,
the last diesel set to rumbling once again,
the last truck transmission resurrected.
To work for fifty years. To work on flivvers,
Studebakers, Jeeps and Macks, to pump gas

in drenching weather, to wheel skull-grinding
Shermans on the clay fields of Aberdeen, to buy
a house, five hundred down, to feed, year in,
year out, a wife and seven kids, to make, all
else failing, a minimum of pensions against

the final ebb. To be at last the overseer
to the "biggest bunch of civil service misfits
you ever saw, out to beat the clock. . .
and me." A proud man whose long dream lay sodden
as the crushed cardboard box on which he worked

beneath the silent trucks, ice clumps from
the snowplow blades dripping in his hearing aids.
To lie shivering there and try and work the goddamned
frozen bolts where the driver'd jammed the steering
gear so he could "park his lazy ass inside."

Year after year of it, until in time he too
came to see the error of his ways and learned
at last not to care so much and not to buck
the system and turned instead to watch
the distant edge of the cold Atlantic beckoning.

He moved closer to the water now and grinned
back at the incessant bitching of the gulls
so like the workers he'd tried to teach to work.
The wind slammed against his windburned face
and shockwhite hair. To his left, still grinding

north and south up Highway One: the big palookas,
bigger than the old Depression rigs he ran
when he was younger, though they still nosed
into wind and fog and storm, those old familiars.
He hummed something he couldn't name and watched

the waves slam their bulk against the shore again.
It made him feel as if the earth itself were trembling
at his feet, as if, besides the billion cubic tons
of sand being even then displaced to north or south,
something might be changed when night had come.

SARCOPHAGUS

Anger so hot, so thick & clotted,
it drowned out even expletives & grunts.
They wouldn't and they wouldn't
oh God they wouldn't

until the tide of blood had risen
to my eyes & I had damned them,
punishing the poor coughing Pinto
all the way to Greenfield to get the lime

myself & saw the two of them
as I shot back into the driveway (denting
the goddamn crankcase as I did it)
cutting the lawn at last: that undulating

seagreen half an acre they said they couldn't
&, no, they wouldn't ever do. *Get out,*
I shouted, *get the hell out now,* as in Masaccio's
expulsion from the garden glimpsed behind

the metal scaffold railing there in the chapel
at Firenze, so that they dropped the rake
& left the mower there mid-swath as I began to lug
the bags of lime myself that squatted

in the trunk like lopped sharks' carcasses
& caught the bag against the indifferent
metal latch, lime exploding over hair
& nose & tongue & unsuspecting eyes,

this cool, sweet, flesh-eating lime,
& put my head against the raised
trunk lid, a clown in white face, at last
defeated by my anger, so that both my sons could see

their father's nakedness as they tread water
out of there, too scared to help, too smart
at least to laugh. Then something deep within
my battered dogbrain whimpered to let go & die,

until a great sargasso frigid briny calm
washed over me & I was slipping
through the makeshift ice hole
into the stunned silence of a bluegreen grey

of ribbed & mottled shapes. No gawky flatfoot
wobblers now, the massive emperor penguins
sleek as ninepins hurtled past me in balletic
arabesque above my head as they skimmed

the underbelly of the floe, indifferent
to my presence. I must have turned, then,
scissoring down into the purple depths
sequestered there to witness squid and horny mollusk,

translucent foetal shrimp, the blue
& phosphorescent spiderforms & worms that palpitate
at zero centigrade plus two: here
at the very edge of life itself

where Dante thought the Mount
of Purgatory rose, the anti-mask
of hell's imploding core, the purple-blackened
bands that signify the depths and then the void.

Far above I caught the airhole icing over,
saw the watching shadow figures who had been
my sons wait until the hole filled in
then turn to other voices calling from the shore.

Alone at last, I stared into those depths
along the spectral edge of twilight and caught

the figure of my father standing at the county
airport gate alone this April, hands folded,

as if rooted, while the twin-engined Beechcraft
labored up & up the unfamiliar purple wetlands
of the Eastern Shore against the coming night
& I waved belated recognition though I knew

he could not see me. *Forgive me father,*
I heard something in me breaking, as now
the lime began to burn the sockets of my eyes.
Forgive me for the grief I know I caused you.

But the depths had grown beyond my telling,
where a face had waited all these many years
drifting in the frigid stillness. It was limewhite
& seemed at home here in the perfect zero cold.

LIGHT STREAMING INTO THE HEAD
FOR VINCE DIMARCO

When the light trickles through the cracked
panel of my son's closed door at 5:00 A.M.
I know he's busy at his books again,
the night watchman waiting for his dawn.
Last week, once he'd gulped his oatmeal down
and driven off to school, I waded through
the clutter of his room, searching for a razor.
Among the thumbed stack of Spanish words,
the strange quadratic symbols, the postcard
pictures of the Last Judgment at Autun
and the Parthenon against the pink dawn eastering,
I found his dog-eared paper Bible beside
a bloodstiff crumpled handkerchief, old signs
I too well know of hours spent searching
in a cell-like room for light to come or come
again while I waited for the niggling words
to kindle into flame. . . .

        I was his age now the first time
I think it struck, though I can see how long
it was in coming, the way my highschool physics
textbook showed the motes swarming in the heated air
until at last they coalesced and flamed, charged
as jaggèd sheets of lightning to leave
the dark forever altered on the stunned mind's eye.
But who at first could have told the difference?
Another day of classes at Manhattan,
the long drive in in traffic and then the long
drive back through twilight autumn drizzle
in my buddy's hearsegrey '57 Ford.

Night after night I would take my dinner
on the rebound then race to make the nightshift
at the Garden City A&P, stacking Krispies,
corn and apricots along the gaping, hungry rows.
Near midnight I'd be home again, my parents
and the younger six asleep, ready
for another round of wrestling with my books.

But this once things were different.
By 3:00 A.M., the tepid instant coffee sloshing
at the bottom of my cup, the radiator wheezing
in the corner like my old asthmatic dog
and the nosebleeds for the moment stanched,
all at once my head went light when Jowett's Plato
gave way to the unexpected music of Ovid's
Metamorphoses, the passage where the boyish
husband turns in dark to find his dear wife
gone and calls out into the indifferent
shadows after her: *Eurydice. Eurydice.*
The cry of the bereft. And then, whether it was
the giddy hour or because I felt my heart
leap at once across some barrier of tongues
which no hell I knew could keep me from,
my hand reached up and touched the tears
forming in the bleary pockets of my eyes
and I felt a light so warm, so very warm
and gentle, like nothing I had ever felt before,
like a golden river flooding through my head.

You know of course how all such rivers sink.
And soon you are looking for the answer
in a bloodstreaked handkerchief, and then
too many cups of coffee and then the metal
ticking clock. Time then to hit the sack.
I staggered to the slanting bathroom sink
and looked into the surface of the giddy

cabinet mirror and splashed my face
and looked again to see the same gaunt
pimply face, the same large nose and lips
and stubbled chin, the untamed hair
still charged and bristling. Only in the eyes
had something changed. . . .

And then the still-fresh
memory of Beacon dying on the sewer-bloated
still majestic Hudson: the sickly river town
where I'd tried to make myself into a priest
and failed. And yet once I'd felt a light
like this —not in myself, of course, not then—
but in the puffy, frog-like eyes of the little
German priest whose name I have forgotten,
a gentle, self-effacing presence whose tiny,
liver-mottled hands had once brushed light
across the dusty shelves which housed he said
his Virgil and his Ovid and that Bunsen flame
Catullus until his eyes had flared, brightening
the dusty room and I had stared, wondering
where all the light was streaming from.

You wait and then you learn to wait some more.
All you can do is turn each empty page, hungry
for whatever light there is, as you try
to blink back the time when something brilliant
flickered blooming in the head. In the meantime
this: that quickening in my own son's eyes,
a river, light, a hope, a something, as when
Plato's dizzy prisoner, as I once heard,
neck bent and groping backwards from his cell
for air, aware of shadows trailing at his feet,
at last looked up to catch full on his face
the staggering honied brilliance of the sun.

· II ·

NEWS THAT STAYS NEWS

I don't know but it might have been
the summer of '58, July, time thickening
or thinning the way heavy fog will on a slick
country road, the headlights spattering
as if they'd hit a wall. What I do remember
though as if it were yesterday is my father

down in the filter room under the pool
at Baumann's Summer Day Camp trying to fix
the leaking chlorine tank and fiddling
with the valves and meters, me standing
on the metal grid ladder over him my hand
on the drum door and then the thick yellow gas

seeping up to catch him staggering sideways
like some Bowery drunk gagging for air as he made it
up the steps his green mouth retching so that
he was straight out for two days. All I caught
was a mouthful of the stuff and that left me
weak-kneed and my lungs rasping, enough of a taste

so it still smells every time I dive
into a motel pool. It was mustard gas killed
my mother's father and don't let anyone tell me
different, though it took fifteen years to do the job,
the cloud hugging the shelled ground as it rolled
in over that no-man's land with the dawn breeze

before it hunkered down on those trapped there
in the trench without their masks. Gas. Gas.
Outlawed in the twenties and then so many times again.
And now, after the Army has at last admitted
to the effects of Agent Orange on our own boys
(to say nothing of what we did to tree and Cong),

the other side is seeding its own rain of terror,
yellow spoilt-grain toxins rocketlaunched by Jeep
and helicopter into Laos and Kampuchea, Yemen
and Afghanistan, dumbstruck villagers including
pigs and babies, left to drown in their own blood,
faces gone black from that internal strangulation,

so that I sit on the edge of my easychair before
the T.V. screen and pound the arm rest
with my clenched right fist, again, again, until
my sons start up, one from his comic book the other
from his world history homework, each wondering
what all this new commotion is about.

THE ASSASSINS

We have come now to expect it at anytime
from almost anywhere: the drugged afternoon
soap, for instance, interrupted for the elemental
drama, live from Dallas, Memphis, New York,
Cairo, Rome. And we know at once what is about

to happen as once again unreels the jerky
footage of the concrete steps, the Texas sky,
the headless shadow at a drunken angle, with always
too much dark or too much light, the crowded
passage leading to the hotel kitchen and the body

lying there, blind eyes flickering, the second
story platform balcony streaked with blood,
the crowd of pilgrims shouting and confused beneath
Bernini's colonnades. Taxonomists of fate,
we keep playing back the shadow on the knoll,

the Harlem stage, the scene beside the park.
A flatbed truck unloads along the jungle's edge.
Another halts before the stand of uniforms
and flashing figures fire into the cameras. One and then
another bpp bpp spurts into the stream of history,

as if they really thought to change its course.
In our time we have had to tell one violence from another
as we replay the real again: the dumdum .22, the steel
jacket spattering the pumpkin skull across the car,
semiautomatic fire and now bazooka rounds.

In our time, too, we have been told, polis snaps
and shrivels like a severed spinal cord. Call it
the hour of the assassin, the century's windfall
fallout, where some mad director keeps playing back
the tape, each time screaming for another name.

29

PENTECOST SUNDAY: HOWARD BEACH

From four on in the pre-dawn summer light:
the Doppler whining of the belly-heavy jets
over Howard Beach, twelve hundred feet above us,
gathering for the steep declension into Kennedy.

I thank whatever powers be, machine or other,
that in the eighteen years I've watched, not one
has hit any of these matchbox cape cod houses,
especially this one, where my brother-in-law,

an ex-New York City cop, his placid wife & my three
teenage nieces live & in summer swim in their big,
delicious aboveground aqua plastic pool
shaded by the pastoral wheeze on one willow

& a silver-speckled maple. Coming into
Kennedy myself I always crane my neck
to see the neat Lionel O-sized brick
& wooden houses against the assorted rectangles,

semi-circles, squares, & rhomboid grids
laid out in the heyday of our early
post-Hiroshima empire style, and try to spot
their house on 87th. Lieutenants, captains,

& chicken colonels flying over Haiphong Harbor
& the outskirts of Hanoi in their splendid
superfortresses, peered like lab technicians
unblinking, steady, through telescopic

crosshair sights bent on bombing runs
of factories, hydro-electric dams
& sometimes even hospitals & no doubt saw
these Platonic shapes repeated. The photos show it

all: how house after house turned ash
as these messengers passed over, whole streets
evaporating like those blips my kids
used to blow away by the millions in the local

video arcades. Sunday morning in the suburbs.
All over Howard Beach people rise up
to let out dogs & cats or put the coffee on,
buy bagels & the *Daily News,* pray

the priest will keep it short on this
the sweltering feast of Pentecost (the roaring wind,
the tongues of fire), so they can hit the beach
before the crowds assemble. Overhead,

in half the time it takes to cook an egg,
a pilot faces east & waits his orders,
the roar of engines forcing tremors on the pinetop
table even as I start up as from a dream

to catch my niece standing in her bathrobe,
the flash of incandescent light expanding
like a frame of overheated film
staring at me as it burns her face away.

LOSS OF LIFE

"A masterpiece of pathos," one eyewitness put it:
the shards of six adults, four children
and two infants, the mesh of bone and eggshell-
shattered skulls embedded in the rockhard lava.
After two thousand years to see how death
caught them huddled in this lower room, the black
magma surging down the mountain to meet the sea,
a molten river eating flesh and hair and eye.

In a wink the river shifts. As when the black flu
swept over all of us: my sons and then my wife
and then myself all one winter's night, so that
for twelve hours we had to inchworm force our faces
from the cooling pools of vomit. And I, pater familias,
lay foetus-shaped across the bedroom floor, right hand
cupped between my legs—as my youngest later told me—
shivering before the quartz heater's ticking glow.

A young man's face flickers on the T.V. screen.
"Many of these tea plants go back a hundred years,
roots as thick round now as, look, my wrists. Surely
Madame Pele does not wish to burn away so much loving
work?" Surely a whistling in the dark, a hundred years
an abacus flick in geologic time, lava flowing
from a thousand glowing fissures. We know she will
take us when she wants. The shadows in the meantime

lengthen. Midnight gathers and prepares to strike.
The runners run now without the hope of winning.
They run because they must against the growing shadows.
Radar-deflecting long-range bombers shudder heavenward
above the hydra-headed warheads hiding in the desert.

Corpus Christi stalks the North Atlantic's waters
on a grid where, when it happens, as one official has it,
"the living will learn to envy the already dead."

Bread, flesh, water, the very air transfigured with
the light, our blue world staggering in a death's head
dance, unable any longer to heal itself as the light
finally eats the source. So we are left with words
as usual: chalkdry bits flaking in the biting solar
winds which stir our words like leaves. The leaves
scatter and the leaves reform. Signs everywhere,
like graffiti on these scorched, deserted walls.

WINTER MEDITATION

And now it's snow again, snow
on top of snow on top of ice,
layer after frozen layer, like
year rings radiating out from logs

stacked against this winter,
like a cross-section of lives
lived out at Ebla, Troy or Jericho:
humus, clay, shard and bone.

Pipes, half-inch copper or inch-
round steel, frozen to the core,
the wind chill factor down
to minus forty, grey skies, then more

precipitation, then plummeting again.
And now, what we all knew was waiting
in the wings: the news of tragedy,
California rain (snow's other form)

upending ten billion cubic feet
of silt, becoming snow as it hurtles up
the eastern seaboard, the record cold
a tidal wave as it rolls across

the northern Rockies, the death toll
rising like those old familiar body
counts used to come from Nam each
Thursday night. Flight 90

out of Washington, Icarus bound
for Miami weather, weighted down
with skin of ice and skin of snow,
takes out half the Fourteenth

Street Bridge, five cars, a truck,
and eighty lives like that, sinking
through Potomac's ice, the weighted
bodies strapped secure in place,

a body bobbing here and there, one
passing the ring to the desperate
others until he too drops out of sight,
Man Number 6, otherwise unknown, salvage

operations stopped by still more snow,
this ash, this gritty sand drifting
on the choked cities and the rivers,
the raised faces finally going under.

16/I/82

ON THE SUBLIME
FOR TERRENCE DES PRES

When Burke stared into the heart of the Sublime
his singed eyes flinched at what he saw. Even
Longinus had it wrong. Terror was at the heart
of it, a sort of noble terror. By way of metaphor
he thought of *écartelèment*, the flesh
torn off and scattered bit by bit, a fitting
end to those who would tear apart the state.

As with us all, it was the ecstasy of suffering
attracted Burke: the way the victim's teeth
grit on edge, the hair flares out, the forehead
puckers like a prune, the eyes roll inward.
Then the voice becomes an animal's, a staccato
series first of shrieks and then of groans,
pain registered in nearly perfect fits.

By way of classic balance, he knew terror
has the same effect on us and that, so long
as we are not the ones dismembered, gives rise
to something like "delightful horror," a tranquil
terror which is but another name for the Sublime.

In the year the Reign of Terror finally struck,
Kant struck back with yet another formulation.
By way of metaphor he chose the raging sea.
When the storm drowns us, he said, it washes
out our shouts. Waves rise and fall and crash
against the cliffs and lightning shakes
our very core. We feel dismembered, bits ready
to be swallowed up in death, until the mind itself
assumes its demon power and *becomes* the storm.

Consider Turner's painting of the burning
of the House of Commons and the House of Lords.
In disbelief the figures clumped together
by the river's edge stare like horses trapped
in burning stalls as flames embrace them, until
the frizzled trees, lung-scorching air, the Thames
itself *become* the flames on which they stare.
The eye stares at the edges of the painter's frame
which cannot hold those all-consuming flames.

Gods that we are, we have our own Sublime
and stare in terror at the pillar of the cloud
billowing high heavenward before our very eyes.
Let there be light, we sigh, light brighter
than ten thousand suns. . . . And suddenly there is.

ULYSSES WEEPS
ON THE TENTH ANNIVERSARY
OF THE PARIS PEACE ACCORDS 1973

It was the song the singer sang
that turned his mind back towards
the walls, the plains, the river
where he had seen the best ones

on both sides go down for good.
He would have liked it better
not to have to think of it again
and so not stir the scarred heart

up once more: the blind pride
of witless senior officers, the mid-
night sorties which had turned
to ambush, the treachery of allies

and the deaths of soldiers he had
had to call the foe. Ten years
already since he'd seen the longed-for
end, and yet the losses had not ceased.

He tried to keep his face hidden
in his cups or in his cloak to shield
his tears, fierce gentle tears he did not
want to shed. But something in the music

of the singer's words welled up within
and burned and healed his eyes. By all
the gods, whatever gods there were
to witness, the past was past, the hacked

defeated bones lay bleaching on the windy
plains, the war itself become the echo
of a rumor, a song . . . and nothing more.
It was enough to have to meet each unsuspecting

dawn, where peacetime seemed as troublesome
as war. His scarred heart could still
count the ridges on his arms and legs
and chest: it was a way of marking time.

But as the singer sang it all came back
again, the same and yet transformed,
so that at first it struck him odd that he
should now delight in raising up his friends

once more from dust to joke and banter
as before, before the sprung shaft stuck
in this one's chest and that one's spine.
He who had been with them all those years

wept now for them and for the others
as for himself, a man without a name who could
still weep for all the nameless dead. Tears fell
because the singing had turned him into song.

A BREAK IN THE WEATHER

Done in and travelling west yesterday
down over the WPA bridge connecting
Sunderland and South Deerfield, on my way
to see the dentist (a tedious half-

terrifying way to spend a morning:
the horse needle filled with novocaine,
the droning highspeed drill, the boring
ride alone) half-past nine and warm enough

to nudge a crocus out of its benumbing
winter sleep, grey swales of greysplotched
grey on grey, erratic windswept drizzle,
the swish swash of milk- and oiltrucks slashed

across my trenchslit vision when, all at once,
out there standing on the midspan of the bridge:
a young man wrapped in a forsythia-yellow poncho
and bearded as some scholar of the Talmud.

Before the Mack truck lumbered splashing
into view, I got to see this place for once—
saw it through another with his eyes shut,
arms bent upward at the elbow, hands cupped up

and rain streaming down his face. There,
just there behind him: the world opening south
to the horizon, unfolding like some giant crocus,
as the clouds swirled stippled grey and white

in bold strokes above the southward
crowding river, as once atop Mount Washington
I remember with winds whipping the glacial scars
and once as I suppose it must have been

those years ago, when horned with radiance,
Moses stood talking with his God. Pilgrim,
stranger, whatever you care to call yourself,
you who stood there above the waters

spelling the Connecticut, my thanks for waking me
to such splendid weather before the traffic
crashed back over us again in torrents
and I lost you in the slanting rearview mirror.

LINES I TOLD MYSELF
I WOULDN'T WRITE

Nebuchadnezzar, von Hoffman the Great, then
Big Sur and Paterson. Instead: since it was
really my kid's dog, we settled for Sparky.
Better than Killer, I guess, better than

White Fang. An onomastic gesture if ever
there was one, more in line with the Ford
pickups sloped to the sides before the town's
one beerstop. And what with Argentine

conscripts freezing in Darwin and Her Majesty's
soldiers leapfrogging the Falklands
out of San Carlo, the *Belgrano* gone
and the *Sheffield* a grave, I promised

myself I wouldn't get soft over one fleabag
arthritic half gone in the head when he didn't
come home. Springtime, we figured, and the old
prunewrinkled groinbag out after women

over in Leverett or up by the lake. But as day
followed day, then a week, then a month,
and his cracked greasy bowl got sacked first
by a tom then by two cranky jays. . . .

There were three nights in there when my wife
kept waking me up, listening for Sparky with each
shift in the wind, the way I remember her doing
night after night whenever one of the babies

got stuck in his breathing. I know I said
I wouldn't go weepy when it came, and I haven't.
At least not that much. Besides, half the neighbors
must be doing a two-step, and the kid who delivers

the papers and used to fling them into the bushes
whenever he heard Sparky can breathe easier now.
And last week a friend put the whole thing
in its proper perspective, reminding me how in Taiwan

and places like that they serve them as delicacies.
So it's over and done with: the backyard service,
the young dogwood planted. . . . Except for this dream,
where an old dog, battered and nettle-flecked, limps

down to the Sawmill. Across its wide waters he sniffs
till he sees us. And though at first he shudders,
he knows he must plunge into that river. When he springs
forth his red coat will glisten. His tail whacks

back and forth, back and forth. As in an Aztec
mound painting caught in the flickering gleam
of the torch, the eyes shift, blend into one.
The lips have curled up. The bright eye shines.

· III ·

In his talk in defense of the muzzle of obscurity that is religion, comrade Bahktin floated up in the clouds or even higher. . . . At some points he did recognize, and even expressed appreciation of, socialism, but he complained of, and worried about, the fact that socialism had no care for the dead (as if there weren't enough services for the dead!), and that, accordingly, in some future time, the people would not forgive us such neglect. . . . Listening to his words one could form the general impression that this entire buried host, reduced to powder as it is, would shortly rise from its tombs and sweep from the face of the earth all the Communists and the Socialism they promote. Comrade Gutman spoke fifth. . . . *(13 December 1918.)*

Q/A

Q. And what was it he felt, first
at first light waking fitfully, again
at dusk with the paper wrapped about
his feet, and yet again at the hour
of the wolf, darkest moment of the night?
What was it he felt swarming in his blood?

A. Molars flattening down from grinding
so much fat and gristle, ground down
from crushing bone and nutmeat, coarsest
grains, each other even when his jaws
went tense, a family habit with the men.

Q. What else?

A.   The micro-continental shift
of upper mandible sliding past the lower,
the bite and grimace worsening with the days,
the trauma to the overworked left side,
speech spilling through the broken cistern
of the mouth, words dribbling from the tongue.

Q. Yes, yes, what else?

A.   Broken hairs retreating
towards the dome, the temples left there
to defend themselves, the careful coiffure
fooling no one, least of all the girls. And
the eyes: capable of scanning motebeams once
suspended in the slant of bronzen-orange sun,
the scented flakes of boxwood tasted by those
eyes. The broken arches, distended. . .

Q. Go on, go on.

A.   . . . distended stomach, that battle
lost for good, the chest hollowing in upon
itself. The world heard now as garble, sounds
played back to him as on a wound-down grainy tape.
The wheezing gasps, the flatulence of air.

Q. Then age?

A.   Age, the age-old story. Or at least
its long precursor, shadow, with his sycophants,
self-pity, soul-sapping weariness. The loss
of inches to one's height, wristbones chalking
and the weakening of grip, the loss of strength,
of spring, at last the loss of even humor.

Q. What then? What resolution or resolve,
what philosopher's handy key, what saving word?

A. Soul braying loud and bravely, the hurl
and scatter of a million wingèd words, plenitude
like the broadcast scattering of seed.

Q. Of course, of course. The imagination
playing with itself again. And when
the skittering words at last refuse to come,
then what, what then? What resolution then?

A.

PALIMPSEST
FOR BRYAN WOLF

When Poe had crossed and then recrossed
the ancient schoolroom floor more times
than he remembered, he understood

at last. His mind's eye saw the leather-
stiffened books lit by the single candle
loom along the range of oaken shelves

like mountains in the high Romantic mode.
He tapped the sweatstained hollow desks,
too many now to count, age-black,

ink-black, and piled high with dogeared
Latin books and Sanskrit as text bore down
on text. In the half light he saw the desks

scarred and then rescarred with names,
dead names aslant of other names as dead,
grotesque shapes designed to hold whatever

"meaning" they could hold, if that was what
one called it. Nor would anything be clearer
in the light of coming day. He knew

that staring at the sun had blinded
Emerson, knew the search, the patient
search for Ur, this transfiguration

of the logos at the heart of things,
was shit, that one might sooner call
one's mouldy father from the grave

as find the patronymic of one's father's
father's father. Poe knew better,
better knew himself. He understood

how terror-riddled is the text
of one's existence, each new page scribbled
helter-skelter Sanskrit in the dark,

the memory gone amuck, the signs beyond
decipher. Take a word, he says,
some common word, and tell it over

over over, until the sound,
by dint of saying, stops saying
anything beyond its selfsame sound,

vox flata, a windy beating of the gums.
He saw that any word at last
was less than met the eye, saw how

the mind's eye straining draws at last
upon the single candle of the self
left to gasp and sputter in the dark.

SOME SORT OF ANSWER

FOR WILLIAM CARLOS WILLIAMS

Three A.M. again: the only light
light leaking from the open door
of the refrigerator. That, and whatever
light the stars could spare as they glinted
through the frost-rimmed kitchen windows.
At last I had caught up with him —
or he with me — as he knelt there searching
for the plums he knew were somewhere.

I'd had ten years and more of it,
and he eight times as much, much of it
spent in shadow. He was still a half head
shorter and half a hundred lighter,
but I could see at once how it was
his elongated shadow I was standing in.
His angry hair was mussed again,
his dark blue vest half open
and his tie a noose around his neck.
It looked as if he'd been up half
the night again, snagging one more kid
from out the dark maternal water.

I was the one to break the silence.
"Well, did I do it? Did you recognize
yourself in what I said?" It was too late now
to foot around with words. I'd earned the right
to get some sort of answer. The bowl of plums
was already in his hand before he answered.
"You dredged up several selves,
I'll give you credit. And, all in all,
you went gentle with the darkness
for the family's sake, though what I did

I had to do. You gave a proper diagnosis,
and I was always one for celebrating light."

I said: "The green glass flares against
the cinders in the back wing of that hospital
because you need it to. And that pink-dyed
Santiago Grove down on the sick Passaic
they finally bulldozed under in the Thirties
was still a place the kids could splash around
in summer, though the cost was high enough.
That was then. The times have changed."

He looked hard at me across his steel-
rimmed glasses and figured what was coming
next. "So you're still not finished
with that scalpel? You want to go on
probing for the heart and brain.
And what good will that do us?
Listen to a story. Swiftfoot Hermes rises
to the surface like a salmon breaking water.
He holds a letter penned in hell.
You read it and you think you understand
and you put your heart at ease
before he yanks the letter back to hell.
So one has told the truth,
whatever that may be, but always
in such figures as we alone will understand."

I started towards him now. "I had to write
my letter once I thought I understood
just what it was you meant to tell
the women and the woman of yourself."

He saw me make my move and he was ready.
"You mean what I told you of *yourself*.
For me it was the woman *in* myself.
Don't palm your troubles off on me.
You think these plums belong to you?

Hell, they go to whoever finds them out
and takes them while they're still
worth eating. Listen up again. Only
in our poems are we ever really us.
And what's a poem? A track of flyspecks
flecked across the paper. Do you think
the parents take the doctor's hand
and kiss it when he breaks the news
about their cancer-stricken kid?
So you spent all these years to learn
the news about me, staring at the print
upon the page until it swam before your
eyes in a million drifting dots. Did you
think you'd ever find *me* floating
in that amniotic ink? Did you really think
you could ever re-create your father?"

By now he'd stuffed the plums into his pockets.
"So we really *were* that close?" I started
as I lunged across the room to hold him.
But he was still too quick for me. With one
swift move he shut the ice-box door, returning
each of us to his old familiar darkness.

THE GHOST

Upland, behind the house itself, behind
the lilacs and the clump of pines, beyond
the upper clearing, he could just make out
the weathered cabin where the old man spent

his final years. Rain swept the half-familiar
pasture and the darkening hills like a buzz
thrumming against the panes. Once more he heard
the half-familiar ghost come sauntering down

to taunt him with its patter on the still air
which was still air only, the strangled cry inside
his skull whenever no bird sang. What had it
cost to come so far north, New York behind him

and the Sound and even western Massachusetts?
The house he stood in now was further north
than any he had known before, each room stark,
foursquare and skewered from the line, when what

he thought he'd wanted was some south, at least
the south of Hartford, Manhattan's south or even
Camden south and south once more to palm trees
swaying in the sundrenched Keys and surely not

this north of flinty rock and flintlock light
aslant in which an old man sauntered down
from the upland clearing towards the house itself.
North for him meant death, the death that comes

with early fall, the death of winter when these
lonely farms lay stranded like so many starving
deer caught in the haunch-high drifts of moonlit
powder, the death of freezing springs, the drafthorse

crashing down in heavy harness, the work left off
unfinished, new seed rotting in the choking mud.
No matter, though. On the upland he could see
the old man coming towards him, as yet a long

way off, though who could say with footfall shifting
in the rising wind. South was what he'd wanted
and north was having none of it. He'd wanted
spring, a spring of fifty years or more

and that meant south. In spite of which he'd kept
moving north, waiting for the old man's steps
as they grew louder on his ear. Walk or wait,
what matter. He knew now north was where he was.

Robert Frost Farm/Ripton
31 July 1983

57

NORTH/SOUTH
FOR BOB PACK

In the long run for both of us
it will be the willow darkening
in a northern twilight
as the dominant key of winter

reasserts itself. As even now
in late August outside this window
the small birds hesitate among
the branches before they arc

their bodies south for the three
days' flight above the darkening
waters. Angel-winged they turn,
before they lock on their own

essential homings. Or, to see it
from your perspective: flight
to a southernmost extreme. Robert,
for whom if not for you

could I feel this bond, your north
anchoring my still-vexed south?
Even these so-called free-verse
lines arc in a double *pas de deux*

pan-foot, goat-foot rocking back
and forth, playing counter
to that granite bass of yours.
You grin that flinty grin glistening

in the wintry air you call
your home now, made native
by the will itself. "You still
dance a little crazy," you say,

"but no cop could say you didn't
toe the line. What *you* have
is a case of free form hurtling
after form. Count yourself among

the blessèd ones who still have
something to go home to." Robert,
who was it warned us both to work
while there was still light enough

to work with, knowing the long night
must needs be coming on? The night:
when all hands must willy-nilly rest,
the last line edging into granite

or the upturn of the wind, the same wind
which turns the feathers of the small birds
up as they chatter in the branches.
They too must sense the great change

coming on and so begin again while there is
still time to test their wings, half shaped
by years of trial and half again by luck, before
they turn at last into the very air itself.

MINNEAPOLIS: AT THE SUMMER SOLSTICE

What martyr's cry quickens our civil blood,
Wolfe Tone's, Parnell's? Whose sacrifice
on a noche triste centuries alive
enables an ultimate homogeneity?

John Berryman

About this northmidwest polis abrupt
the plane had dropped me in I thought & yet again
I thought. Five days, five full days *and* nights
I tried spying out its soul or, if not *that*
imperious Emersonian immensity, then at least

some centering primal nucleus of riverbed or track.
Minneapolis: a mishmash appellation half Greek/half Sioux,
flat anomaly of broad boulevards & concrete looming granaries
& spiffy, dutiful, high-polish-boots police.
And yet: like oatmeal after Venice's canals,

the ducal stone of Florence, rococo Rome, without even
slum Dublin's gorgeous Georgian doors. No, *this*
was not so very unlike New World Syracuse and Rome
or, even closer home: a 91-beribboned Springfield,
home of basketball and the repeating rifle.

Except for old New York and maybe Bourbon Street
Orleans & the quaint grey quais of palmetto-laced
old Charleston, the post-blue highway cities
of America, let's face it, are like this.
It took chutzpah to build Paterson from those old

rejected stones, the which Doc Williams pretty much
avoided, I see better now, for the far more interesting
issue of himself. There are no holy cities in America,

at least none *this* side of the border, north
or south. No Quebec shrine, no maternal Guadalupe,

no Czestochowa, Zurich, Canterbury, Rome,
and surely no Kyoto. No angel's wing to brush sacred
mosques or crypt or wall: that painted golden light
which has stood four thousand years for blessed Jerusalem.
Ah, if the tonsured fathers of the companie of Francis

could see L.A. or San Francisco now, how they'd
slap their fevered brows. And yet here I was: one more
exhausting pilgrimage to go, twenty pounds the lighter,
the trick of leaning into the fiery furnace
until my eyelids curled & singed as once

with Ananaius, Azarius & the others. Minneapolis:
this phoenix singer's final nesting place, the exhausted
martyr's star upon those expansive coalpiers that skirt
the adolescent Mississippi, star glinting in the rubble
from that morning when he tilted out & leapt.

Ah, who could write like him, count poem for blessèd
poem? the whirlwind polyvalvèd bellow of that deeply
wounded man who builded him an altar to outlast plastic
food & foodstands & exfoliating lots, the city over which
he'd brooded, this swarming vital northern desolation.

THE SIGN

Crazy little momma comes a-knockin'
Knockin' at mah fron' door, door, door
Crazy little momma comes a-knockin'
Jes lak she did before . . . .

"May the Fates conspire to lift my clamant voice
here on this sacred mountain & may they bestow
upon this woman who is my wife an unambiguous sign
that I too have every priestly right
to be spokesmanwomanperson for the womonfyre
poems of Rich as for any other poet."
And that was what I said as I strode out into the sun.

As usual, my wife was still three steps ahead of me
& walking towards the car parked behind the Shaker-
style schoolhouse where we were living,
in the midst of quipping something about
the different readings anyone would have
if *they* could spend a day with Mr. Highpriest,
the self-proclaimed clairvoyant pupil of the central

golden eye, when all at once pulsating
supernovas boinged off flashing in my head.
Thus the sign I'd called aloud for had been granted
when the dormant toolshed that had hunkered
there behind that schoolhouse a hundred years & more
at once reared up to unveil a starry cosmic night
like some visionary etching out of Blake & I was rolling over

on the grass to keep from blacking altogether out.
By then Eileen had turned, wondering why
her husband kept flipping over on his side and back
the way our weird old mongrel dog would do whenever

he went crazy snapping after noxious ticking fleas.
Ah, what had the tough old goddesses in store?
She got a cold wet cloth & wrapped it gently

on my scalp then helped me stagger to my feet
as I watched in giddy disbelief the unexpected sign
turn martyr's red. There was the other woman
too, the young, no-nonsense nurse named Laurie,
close enough in name I thought to Petrarch's noble Laura
& the memory of those Eugenian scented sepia-tinted hills
seen once at dusk, & both had steadied him

to get the dazzled prophet down & off his sacred mountain
as the ambulance tracked the winding east branch
of the Middlebury River down into town. So here he was,
crumpled in the back seat, his pulse still climbing
up Mont Blanc as he mumbled arrant nonsense
he was sure was oracle itself. There would be other
women at the hospital, capable of taking care

of him quite well, thankyou, he was made to understand,
without his interfering hands, alone. Which was,
he also understood, perhaps his deepest fear:
that indeed they *could* do just as well without him.
Ah, but could *he* without them do?
"May the goddesses conspire," he hears Mr. Highpriest
mutter to himself, the blood plume dripping in his eyes,

"may they conspire to fill my life with such women
& their music & their touch, their sanity . . . & care.
Help me read aright plus positive this elemental sign
as from the Fates as a paratoxic good. In the ancient war
of man & woman may someday there come peace & yes
a common language and with it women's laughter . . . & let
the gentle Fates come knocking with a little more panache."

CLEANING OUT THE CELLAR

Time once more to clean the cellar out,
to thin the brace of cataleptic bikes,
the moldy bats and gloves, the brown-edged news,
the cardboard boxes stacked in grainy light:
things kept against a time which never comes.
Like those mummy notebooks bloated
with my dead professors' gnomic axioms.
So much *angst* expended once
on the dusty air of accident and form.
The cellar holds its mummy time intact:
a box of old tax ledgers, a disassembled wheel,
one chipped claw hammer and three large nails,
this cookie tray of broken Christmas bulbs,
my lost dog's cracked green plastic supper bowl
kept these eighteen months in case his bones
should ever lope their jaunty way back home.

In this flyblown print of Dürer's *Melencolia*,
each thing sits apart, insists on keeping
to itself. An angel twiddles with a large
twin iron compass, sideways glowers
at a falling star. The scales clink empty
in the breeze above his head. Each broad
surface of the granite polyhedron, whether in
or out of shadow, insists *I am, I am,*
I am, as sand sifts down the hourglass
and dust seems to measure dust.
A batfaced serpent, mouth agape, grips
its needle teeth about the word:
the mirror meaning of the melancholy whole.

A seawracked, seascummed catalogue
of things to number on the fingers
of the mind, then lug grunting up
the cellar steps to cart the load away.
O blessèd Abelard and good St. Freud,
subtle masters of the windy sound,
O you who understood how words
were thresholds of the terrible sublime,
the inverted image dancing in the lake,
in the final count worth a trunk
of tens and twenties minted Richmond,
April, 1865, *if* you can hear me
as you circumambulate about the brilliant
dark as if at ease at last,
the word a dream of dancing things,
the dream become the dancing Word itself,
remember me as rooting in my cellar,
counting on my fingers and my toes.

·IV·

GOODNIGHT IRENE

I am ten and a half and my father
has let me come to work with him again
at Scotty's Esso in Mineola, the wood
and plaster tudor building three blocks
east of the pseudo-bauhaus boy's
Catholic highschool, from which one day
I will venture out to try the priesthood on
(and fail) knowing it is not
for me when I start keeping (against
Brother Clyde's injunction) a marker
in my physics textbook beside the picture
of the lovely in the armlength cashmere sweater
with those swelling upturned breasts.
And from beneath the row of fanbelts
hanging spiderlike I can see the neon
Rheingold sign pulse dully in the doorway
of the Colonial Bar & Grill
where thirteen years from now Wilbur
will split my upper lip with an ice cube
flung across the smoky underwater room
before my brother Walter can hit him
easy with that cross-body block of his
while I reel off my drunky speech to these
my friends a week before my marriage.
But for now I am inside the station
listening to my father singing chorus
after chorus of "Irene, goodnight, Irene,
I'll see you in my dreams," seeing only
part of his face down in the grease pit,
the wrench in his clenched right fist,
his hooded lamp throwing fitful shadows
all across the wall, as he performs
whatever mysteries it is he does to cars.
Useless even to my father, I watch

the yellow sunlight blocked in squares
drift east across the blackened bench
where two halfmoon brakedrums cup
the ballpeen hammer as in a Juan Gris
still life, the calendar (gift of *Kelly's
Tires*) still turned to August, above which
the cellophane with the nightie
painted on it conceals the underlying
mystery of the lady kneeling there
who smiles frankly at me.
And now the warm smell of leaking
kerosene from the thumbsmeared
darkgreen fifty-gallon tin as I wipe
the opaque bluegreen bottles
of reconstituted oil for the old
"baraccas" as my father calls them.
On the box radio above the wheezy Coke machine
word drones Marines are fighting in a place
called Seoul but there is trouble even
closer home and soon someone is singing
once again the song my father
also loves to sing, "Irene, Goodnight."
And I think of mother back in Levittown
teaching Walter how to read
as my sisters go on playing dolly,
the younger one putting her wedding dress
on backwards while I help my father
put all the bolts into one coffee can
and all the nuts into the other.
And now my Uncle Vic (the one
the strokes choked off three years ago)
grabs his grease-clogged rag
and mutters as he strides out
into the sun to gas up some revved-up Ford,
the static gurgling high above the engine's
macho rumble while my father goes on working
on the underbelly of the car

70

where the light is coming from,
singing still again "Goodnight, Irene."
But my mother's name is not Irene
her name is Harriet and I wonder why
my father wants to see this other lady
in his dreams but I cannot ask
and will not even know what it is
I want to ask until I am older
than he is this September afternoon in 1950
and now the tears well up for him
and for my mother and myself as I turn
to look back down into the empty pit
to tell him now I understand.

THE RING

Only after, wading waist deep
through the black waters of the duck pond,
did he feel its absence first: the slight
pressure on the small finger of his right
hand gone. He would have lost it, then,

in tumbling from the peak of the covered
bridge in the shoot-out re-enactment
staged in the brilliant outdoors light
for those seven hundred spellbound
daycamp kids. He would have lost it

in the mud pushing up for air, the fall
and death of the Outlaw convincing to the kids
and to himself for the minute he was under.
Sport enough for a watermelon sort
of afternoon. But this was deadly earnest.

Forget the macho saga of the West, his boss
swinging that pearl-handled gun of his,
forget his foreman father shouting
from the stand of willows above the pond
to load the garbage truck before the dump

in Oceanside closed down. Instead he'd turned
back to the little pond, scattering
the quacking ducks, diving under time
and time again to claw at stringy weeds
and slimy rocks as he sifted for the little ring.

And so — long after the kids and counsellors
were gone and night had drifted in and he had
to give it up and tell her, though day by day,

painting fence or cleaning up the trash — he kept
staring at the pond, puzzling where the little thing

could be. Twenty years and more and that girl
his wife now and mother of their three tall sons
and still it troubles him, that highschool ring,
Mary Louis, Class of '59, a thing
worth maybe sixty bucks (if that)

at the present gold exchange, an accident
as both of them had come to understand. Forget it,
she had said, and that seemed that. . . . Except
as sign, except as something lost in that
mock-heroic falling from a height

into the duckslime water, a *prefigura*, sign
circling on itself. He might have shrugged it off,
this husband and this dedicated father, after all
the mediating years. Except, that is,
for the bent figure he sees wading wet and cold

out into the water with the evening shadows
coming on. For the hundreth and the thousandth
time he watches as the figure holds its breath
and he feels his heart begin again to pound
as he goes under one more time. His eyes

tear and his fingertips are raw
from clawing as he circles still again,
searching for the thing he cannot name
inside the little ring which would surely
hold the answer if only he could find it.

THE TERN'S EYE
FOR EILEEN

By slow degrees
the eye defines anew
the world cast up each morning
by shifting wind and sea. As now,
where eight, then nine,
then ten terns peck
the too bright whiteness
of these brinebleached sands
along the southeast tip
of Florida. Aware
and wary, the terns
define the shadow first
and then the foreign substance
before they skitter,
twisting stiff heads left
and right then left again
like one-eyed Jacks, scattering
unwitting Sanskrit tracks
across the sand.

The tern's unblinking eye
is jack and king and queen
in a world no man
will ever understand and moves
this way and that
before the sea's
encroaching endless step.
The patient lifting rising
falling patient ebbing
rocks us at last to sleep each night
but when we wake we wake
to hear again those cries.

74

But do those cries
make even half
the sense a tern's track makes
across the ceaseless shifting sands?
And if we say
such things as these
cry out
which of us can say
we understand them?

Yet
when we cry out
do our cries mean any more?
And if they do to whom?
For months, now, years,
I have tried to make it work
upon the page: some image,
some simple image I hoped
could track my meaning down.
But like the Sanskrit
of the tern's configurations
I have skittered arabesques
even as I backtracked
back & forth
across the page,
caught in the cross fire
of a cross wind
between what I said
and what I meant to say,
all of it at last a fist
of beachblown sticks
I could not
keep from shifting.

So now I must try again
to watch with shifting eyes
a thousand miles from home
the terndart in your eyes

75

as you read this letter.
My dear, my darling one,
I know you are a woman
and a woman has a tern's eye too
which opens inward on a world
where she must be the final reader.

Like the scumbled signs the sandtern leaves,
a woman leaves her track in Sanskrit,
like the track of any man.
For in the world
which she and she alone defines
she makes such meanings
as she knows she must.

The short
and long of it is that she reads
the beachblown seastraw sticks
and knows
the world in them not
as the sticks have said
but as she knows the world is.

THE LURE
WORDS FOR MY GODSON, EIGHTEEN HOURS OLD

What is this strange translucent light
come coursing through this heaving
bonecage to make it rise and fall
and why is this cord through which
I fed and sucked in air these weeks
and months now brown and disconnected?
What are these sounds which ebb
and then return so unlike the winedark waters
where eye gave sprout potato-like
and ear and heart and spongy lung?
And have I only dreamt those sun-blessed
goldgreen islands where giant
songdrenched turtles drift forever?

Whose is this voice this face which leans
in shadow murmuring above me
and whose this other's like a distant foghorn
off the North Atlantic coast as he lifts
me like a wave? What was it drew me
near and nearer until with wail
I entered naked new hands flailing out
and will I ever learn to navigate
this saffron light or understand
the name the shadows here above me
keep throwing out like bread on water
while this mouth of mine agape and gasping
keeps trying to return their distant calls?

PRIME MOVER

FOR BILL HEYEN

In this small painting of Virgin and Child
Geertgen used the old mandorla
to order his world, the arclight yellows
fanning out towards the ends of the picture
into infra-red dark.

Three tiers of angels float
in a clockwise spiral, those closest
to the Word bathed
in a sea of silent adoration,
too too happy for utterance itself.

In the second ring are twelve angels,
each with an instrument of the passion,
the tortured notes within the major sea.
Here are the spikes, the cross,
the studded whip and the pillar, the spear

to probe the very secret of the heart.
In thirty years this Jew will die
for "ragioni di stato," for reasons of State.
In the outermost circle, the artist has doubled
the number of angels who blare out in wonder

the news of the ages in a heavenly music
of which, however, the reader can hear nothing.
One plays a lute, another a bagpipe,
another a horn, a shawm and a clapper,
even a clavicytherium of sorts,

if the eye is not deceived.
Dante spoke of just such celestial concerts,
as if he'd witnessed one himself.

78

So too Aquinas and the pseudo-
Areopagite, who read this scene

to mean God's word once sang
the world into being. In his time too
Geertgen felt the need to sing
his re-enactment of the word
which dances in us all.

From what we can see,
even this minor & forgotten artist
learned enough before he died
at twenty-eight to try a major harmony
of light dancing out in giddy swirls

from the central Absence
of the almond-scented, almond-shaped
mandorla five hundred years
before we moderns found ourselves
adrift and hurtling through this post-

Holocaust, post-Hiroshima void
we have had to learn to call our home.
At the heart of the painting
a little boy twists from his mother,
feet flailing out this way and that.

And if she did not hold him tight
he would surely hurt himself on the sharp edge
of the crescent from which she too
now seems to perch precariously.
In each hand the child jangles a bell,

just like the street urchin angel
he watches. Among all the bleats
and the twangs and the curious quavers,
the tweet and the fleedle
and the tum-te-tum-tums, the first

(tentative) jangle as the Prime Mover
begins to play out word after word
in unending tempo. The street urchin
watches, then plays the Word jingle
for jangle as now all the angels

pick up his lead and the Void
begins swelling with music, a wondrous
symphony of which we can hear nothing.
For that is how the wordless Word
is said to move among His creatures.

·V·

THE EASTERN POINT MEDITATIONS

It was during this time that a serious disturbance broke out in connection with the Way. A silversmith called Demetrius, who employed a large number of craftsmen making silver shrines of Diana, called a meeting of his own men with others in the same trade. "As you men know," he said, "it is on this industry that we depend for our prosperity. Now you must have seen and heard how, not just in Ephesus but nearly everywhere in Asia, this man Paul has persuaded and converted a great number of people with his argument that gods made by hand are not gods at all. This threatens not only to discredit our trade, but also to reduce the sanctuary of the great goddess Diana to unimportance. It could end up by taking away all the prestige of a goddess venerated all over Asia, yes, and everywhere in the civilized world."

Acts, 19:23-28.

We are always willing to fancy ourselves within a little of happiness and when, with repeated efforts we cannot reach it, persuade ourselves that it is intercepted by an ill-paired mate since, if we could find any other obstacle, it would be our own fault that it was not removed.

Dr. Johnson

i

November 5th: Monday night

In shadow, in late light breaking only now
beneath the pied, the piled clouds behind me, a milksoft
moon before me lifting, nearly full and pale, bluepurple
and translucent wafer, heaven's bread suspended

as I raced east along the northern route,
straining to read the dark lines of the map
beside me in the empty seat, intent upon a silence
ripped jaggèd by the sweep of rigs and the patter

of unsteady rain, towards the Eastern Point
retreat house and so away as quickly as I could
from lives I'd left in shambles, not knowing
even now how little I had known myself

or my wolf-fanged lust for doe flank, breast & vulva,
not even caring this time round that I was leaving
what had taken twenty years to build, having kept
guard over my mate & three mancubs day in day out

with an angry jealous fevered eye, a half-crazed timberwolf
loping through a silverdrunken moonscape out now wholly
for himself. I caught the flash of nippled globe & buttock
fleering in the headlights as I entered Gloucester,

searching for the lighthouse. *If you want the goddamn desert,*
for God's sake go alone, my oldest son had stuttered
through clenched teeth, embarrassed for the man he called
his father, streaked cheeks glinting from the lights there

in the highschool parking lot, the neutral ground
I'd chosen where I thought I could "explain." And now,
alone in dark again, past shrouded houses and the waters
all about me, in silent, fumbling prayer, the buzzing

honeysuckle scent of estrus still about me,
I tried to find my way back through clamant foghorns
and the rise & fall of harbor bells to try & piece together
the world I had lifted high to smash against the rocks.

ii

November 6th: Tuesday dawn

Three large ravens flew low across my line
of vision, left to right, before they came to rest
in the wintry branches of a sycamore last week
while I was racing west to get somewhere distracted.

They seemed to want to mean, mean something,
with a down derry derry down down
as they stropped their horny beaks against the wood
and cawed, their blueblack glinted eyes upon me.

And now, again, a hundred miles east, they scold
the damp grey air and stalk the autumn yellow grass,
strutting right to left across the window of my room
with the cocksure arrogance of Kurosawa's bandits.

And the mind unreels once more the image of a boxer
as he crashes to the drunk and unresisting canvas.
The crowd jeers as he tries to clear his clouded,
cotton-heavy brain while the highrumped victor

struts back to his corner. In disbelief he tries
to push up on his unsteady knee & forearms, thinks
he is rising even as his body tilts and crashes sideways
to the giddy mat once more. And the dreaded dream returns:

all afternoon we have held them off, my wife and I, loading
and reloading, our children hidden safely somewhere
in the hold. Though we are near exhaustion, our nerves
and fingers raggèd, still, we have somehow kept the enemy

from boarding. Then, without warning, & suddenly, without
warning, I turn and face her, lift the revolver aimed
point blank at her chest, fire, then watch the jaggèd flesh
of her aorta explode into my face. For a moment I can even

taste the shock of disbelief and then the other shock
of final recognition as her body slumps away. Even my enemies
are stunned by my achievement. Then they start to clamber over.
I hail at last what I have always feared the most.

iii

November 6th: Tuesday morning. 11:30 A.M. Election Day

Deep calls to deep. Down the dark hall to Father Drury
in his study, under the low lamp waiting. He listened
while I forced it trembling out, eyes averted, said nothing
till I'd finished. *Two women, father, I know you understand,*

need to sort things out, "accommodate" these ladies
to a complex, necessary situation. I watched my left hand,
palm up and half-extended, slip down as I raised the right
in compensation. He looked tired, as if he'd heard it

86

all before, scratched something on a little slip of paper,
an *I* then *S*, a passage from Isaiah.
Sit still long enough to read this in your room,
is all he said, then showed me to the door.

It was least what I'd expected, this matzoh, bitter bread,
hard to chew & harder still to swallow: *"Your safety lay*
in Me. But you, you wanted none of it. 'No,' you said,
'I will flee on horseback.' So be it. Flee. AND, you add,

'on wheels, swift wheels.' So be it. Your enemy is
even swifter." Didn't anyone understand where I
was coming from? I'd given twenty years, had wound up
in the intensive care unit of some provincial hospital

with nurses watching as my heartbeat bounced upon a screen.
Give me life, a little summer with a girl, good food & sex
& talk of Bach & Barthes & Motherwell, a little
Dostoievski, & not the faulty burner, not the kids' tuitions,

the bills, the bills, the daily round of things.
And Isaiah: *"Flee, then, till you become a flagstaff*
clacking in the wind, a blown-out beacon, scarecrow
on a stick. And I will still be waiting for you, ready

to lift you & take pity. When you have tasted the dull
& bitter bread of what you've done, then you will begin
to understand." Paperwhite, little slip of wafer, crumpled
nuntius trembling in my hand, how is it, bitter as you were,

you began to taste like the *pandolce,* as at Genoa
when the pink azaleas blossomed in the brisk, rinsed
eastering air, a gift I stuffed into my pockets to carry
half a world away & home to share it with my family?

iv

Wednesday morning. 11:00 A.M. Eastern Point Lighthouse

Having knelt, having paced this tiny camphor-scented cell
with its squeaking cot, its sink, its undistinguished
crucifix, having prayed & pored over the meaning
of the words until my eyes & heart were stinging,

I bundled up & walked down to the lighthouse at the Point.
Then step by halting step along the narrow breakwater
whose chiselled granite rocks had the massive strength
I remember at Fort Sumter when we took the kids to see it

hunkered in the stormy bay at Charleston, imposing
and unyielding, which the blue advancing waves
of Union troops had never breeched. The wind from off
the North Atlantic was howling still, as if

it might sweep me up and hurl me off the edge
against the jutting rocks until my broken body sank
beneath the waters. Still, I kept walking further out,
only feet above the churning spittle of those rising waters,

keeping to the narrow surface with its fresh pools
of yellow-green gull droppings, out and further out
until at last I reached the end. . . .
There was nothing now before me but the final edge

and the snarling greyblack water. I thought of Hopkins
on his last retreat at Tullabeg, in his forty-fifth
and final year, my age exactly now, a good man
already broken, who in six months would be dead.

"The question is," he wrote, afraid, "how
do I advance the side I serve on?" Which way
lay the way? Then I remembered something I had heard
from Mark at Mass the evening before:

88

Come away to some lonely place all by yourself
and rest there for a while. So here is where it ends,
no symbol but the very thing itself in the slapping waves
below. When I begged You for some answer, something

I could build on, all you gave me was an image
of a broken body. Cold comfort, that. Ah, but it was You
who also wrapped me like a blanket in your peace. Besides,
where else could I go? Having wandered out this far,

I turn, fumbling with my brinesmeared glasses,
and catch back in the distant unexpected brilliance
once again the spit of sand atop which hunkers there
unyielding & unmoved: a tiny lighthouse with a beacon.

v

November 8th: Thursday evening. Nightfall.

Maranatha: Sit still & learn to wait for him
to come in his own good time. So, after the talks, after
the Ignatian exercises, after pacing in the confines
of my cell, knowing there was a more-than-human drama

to be witnessed in the rising of the full moon
which would lift in bright arpeggios above Cape Ann
at twenty-five past four, I left my room at low tide
to walk out to the skull-shaped outcrop they call Brace Rock,

hopskipping over the angular granite slabs, the seaweed,
kelp, this volcanic upthrust, until at last I scuffled up
the seagull-guanoed rose-sepia-tinted rocks foot by foot
to the highest point, anxious to greet my sister moon alone.

But those lizard-grey chameleon clouds, which till now
I had not distinguished from the sea, stretched east
and down to the horizon. And so the moment I had waited for
in the pop-Romantic Bierstadt theatre of my mind

swept past without event. Once more I was made aware
the waves were pounding still against the rocks below,
bleeding with the salt-commingling darkness of the air.
Behind me, to the west, I caught lights in the retreat house

coming on, one by one by one. *Go back*, the waters
whispered, gnashing, *or be cut off from the mainland
and the others. Go back.* I understood then, groping
for a foothold down the dark-encrusted rocks,

that I would have to wait until the dark got even darker
before I would begin to see the light.
Not the *schola intellecta*, Fr. Drury says. It is
an issue rather of the *schola affecta*. That is,

it is not a "doctrine" we are after but a human being,
the schooling of the heart. Then he pointed to the bloodless
body on the cross. *This is your example of kenosis,
the emptying of yourself to fill up others.*

The dark paradoxes pound against the temples of my skull.
In chapel, in darkness now, as one more shadow bent among
the shadows, I glimpse the flicker of the sanctuary lamp
as it sets the shadows dancing on the wall, my own among them,

and suddenly I am happy. For the first time in months I have
finally come to rest. Out the crazed & frosted window panes
I catch the moon rising there at last. She rises clear above
her ashes, gold gathering against the pulsing velvet black.

November 9th: Friday afternoon. 3:00 P.M.

A bowl of hot corn chowder, a piece of bread, an orange.
I picked up two white woolen blankets from the chest
& walked down to the rocks I'd come across that morning
out beyond one of the neglected garden paths which criss-

cross this old estate. I was Alice in the garden,
discovered long-necked bottles from a picnic lunch left
these sixty years, inching down into the unresisting dank
& spongy moss, walked through the ruined tennis courts,

roots of scrub-oak, pine, and seaplum breaking up the clay.
Again I saw an image of the path which I had chosen when,
a frightened kid of twenty-three I took her for my wife,
a girl of twenty-one, to trek together through underbrush

& clearing, in time taking three sons into the ruined garden
with us. I thought of how I'd tried to change halfway
through the journey & make it work with words: the Mad
Hatter's mad American soliloquy. I understood now

that all of that was finished, that there was work at home
to do. The wind was nearly screaming when I found my way
out of the garden. Waves were crashing now against the worn,
resisting rock. At the sea's edge in a light so strong

you could have cupped your hands & caught it I sat
like an Arapahoe, wrapped up in my blankets, and stared out
at the terrifying magnitude of waters. Three gulls swept
across my line of vision left to right, playing

the prevailing eastern wind with outstretched wings
as they searched the sea for food. Then they circled
into the wind till they were back where they had started,
staring from the rock where I had stood the night before.

I sat still as the wind whacked against my ear in the chill
& brilliant day and waited. Only when the noise had pitched
itself to silence did I catch the whisper, warming me
& comforting, until I could contain myself no longer,

but thought I understood & so began to sing
what words I could remember of the Abba Father
as I'd heard it from the children in the makeshift choir
back in Turners, words of the potter, words of the clay.

And reached out arms to embrace the blue-bright
mothering air everywhere around me while I tried
to keep my hat from sweeping off & down into the vortex
of the yelping sea below. Then I was crying.

The Inuit know the journey to the Land of the Dead
is long & cold & dark. Which is why they clothe
their dead with extra furs and sealskins & line
their boots with the short summer's precious grasses.

vii

November 10: Saturday morning. 3:00 A.M.

And the dream of going home returns. The mind's rehearsal
of the longed-for, dreaded going home against the odds.
The watching, the watching & the waiting, the way
a wife will watch a reformed unsteady alcoholic husband,

kitchen & bedroom become a stage, the pitiful domestic
modern comedy, voice rising to a strained falsetto pitch,
forced laughter at the inconsequential misdirected joke,
the getting on with it, as if nothing had transpired,

when she & you & your boys know now in some terrifying
fundamental way that everything has changed. . . .
Shipwrecked Ulysses waits green-eyed for the suitors.
He is sullen, out of shape, & must struggle with his bow

to string it. He reaches for an arrow from his quiver,
cuts his finger on the barb, then aims it at the suitor
only he the canny one in his hallucinations sees. . . .
He hears the phone ring, waits for his wife to pick it up,

listens, waits. . . . He is confused, wonders what the duties
of a father who has left his sons can be, wonders if his sons
will listen. And yet his spirit knows he has been blessed
beyond belief, knows from his phonecalls home these last

two days the sense of strained relief he's heard there,
his wife's familiar talk of friends, of relatives
who miss him, want him home. It is a counting off of beads
to form a story, two decades told already, spliced once more

as he puts together how his sons have carried on. It is,
he sees, the age-old narrative of endless petty problems
& of consolations which will end he hopes now only
with his death. But with it comes the staggering giddy sense

that he is needed, if to fix the sink, then a chance to help
his sons, & if that to be taken once more into confidence,
& perhaps in time back into her arms. The woman: the one
who would not listen when they counselled her to leave you,

let the bastard go, the fire-tempered mettle of a strength
like that, her promise kept to go it with the one she'd chosen
when she'd said, as I had too, for better or for worse,
words seared into my blood till even I could not avoid them.

93

viii

November 10th: Saturday morning. 7:30 A.M.

:Like a fading coal, which some invisible source,
some ever-shifting wind, awakens to a momentary brilliance.
In this the poem, the prayer and love are one,
for like the fading embers all must wait upon the wind.

The self, the conscious self calls this truth
by many names as, afterwards, an irritant, those pressures
which can be contained no longer and so burst forth
into the cry of words. I am afraid of my own self.

I am the drunk the morning after who, seeing
the smashed headlight, the splattered blood and clumps
of hair still frozen to the grill, wants nothing more
than to forget, and so staggers back inside

into the pantry to "brace" himself by looking
for another shot of amber-tinted whiskey, a beer,
a drop of cordial, a goddamn can of sterno, *anything.*
The logs crackle in the dark oak tudor central fireplace

on this the final morning. The screened-in fire recedes
to smoldering embers, except when the wind rattles
for a moment in the chimney. *Maranatha.* Come, Lord,
let your fire consume this fire, until the grate is empty

but for the final sift of ashes. . . .
In silence, in smoldering cold drizzle after breakfast,
I walked out through the gates down to the stippled pond.
A blue heron fed among the shallows.

Stunned by its unexpected beauty, I stood stock still
and stared, until, sensing me at last,
sensing an intruder on its world, it lifted slowly
with an unforced grace just feet above the water,

94

flapping its gorgeous blueblack wings, rising
in an arc before it left my field of vision, though not
before I'd glimpsed the greys, the rainbow blues,
the warm pink haze it had harbored on its breast.

ix

November 10th: Saturday. Noon. Departure.

Then the silence of the extraordinary faces, Merton wrote
a week before his death, the huge and subtle smiles
of the Buddhas there in the monks' enclosure at Polonnaruwa,
gaiety exploding from the very rocks themselves.

O Lady of Good Voyage, remember me in the shoals
and in the insidious undercurrents especially,
when the undulant, swaying eelgrass like softest
hair begins hissing once more sweetly, the sunken self

lulling lovesongs to itself. Blessèd was your womb
when the unborn babe, the harbinger your cousin carried
leapt for joy, as once David leapt for joy,
a king dancing naked round and round for drunken joy

before the sacred ark. Help me too to hear his word
when most I need it and least want to hear and keep it.
Help me in the coming storms to more than merely mouth
the mantra of the one barely possible annunciation.

Here on these rocks which face into the full
& unimpeded force of the North Atlantic
I have come this one last time to sing your praises.
Hosanna, the eye cries out in silence, hosanna

in the highest, as the advancing waves crash once more
against the tympanum of rocks in a dithyrambic chorus
you think you have begun at last to understand.
In the great & terrifying dialogue with love,

you know many women have helped you find
the woman in yourself. There are many paths
in the singing underbrush you might have followed.
But as with any maze it is the center that you seek.

There is only one you can go home to. So now it is,
after all these many years, the moment to begin again,
to listen as if it were the first day in the garden
to the woman who has waited all these years for you

to finally see her. Not mere apostrophe and not the screen
of metaphor, & not the mediation of the logos only. Now
you will have to learn to stand naked there before her,
to stand there as you are, as the figure that you are.

5 November 1984—3 February 1985

THEN SINGS MY SOUL

Who can tell a man's real pain
—or a woman's either— when they learn
the news at last that they must die? Sure
we all know none of us is going anywhere

except in some pineslab box or its fine
expensive equal. But don't we put it off
another day, and then another and another,
as I suppose we must to cope? And so

with Lenny, Leonardo Rodriguez, a man
in the old world mold, a Spaniard
of great dignity and a fine humility,
telling us on this last retreat for men

that he had finally given up praying
because he didn't want to hear
what God might want to tell him now:
that he wanted Lenny soon in spite

of the hard facts that he had his kids,
his still beautiful wife, and an agèd
mother to support. I can tell you now
it hit us hard him telling us because

for me as for the others he'd been
the model, had been a leader, raised
in the old Faith of San Juan de la Cruz
and Santa Teresa de Avila, this toreador

waving the red flag at death itself,
horns lowered and hurling down on him.
This story has no ending because there is
still life and life means hope. But

on the third day, at the last Mass, we were
all sitting in one big circle like something
out of Dante—fifty laymen, a priest, a nun—
with Guido DiPietro playing his guitar

and singing an old hymn in that tenor voice
of his, and all of us joining in at the refrain,
Then sings my soul, my Savior God to thee,
How great thou art, how great thou art,

and there I was on Lenny's left, listening
to him sing, his voice cracked with resignation,
how great thou art, until angry glad tears
began rolling down my face, surprising me. . . .

Lord, listen to the sound of my voice.
Grant Lenny health and long life. Or,
if not that, whatever strength and peace
he needs. His family likewise, and

his friends. Grant me too the courage
to face death when it shall notice me,
when I shall still not understand why
there is so much sorrow in the world.

Teach me to stare down those lowered horns
on the deadend street that shall have no alleys
and no open doors. And grant me the courage
then to still sing to thee, *how great thou art.*